World Art

Sue Nicholson

QED Publishing

Copyright © QED Publishing 2005

First published in the UK in 2005 by
QED Publishing
A Quarto Group company
226 City Road
London EC1V 2TT

www.qed-publishing.co.uk

A Catalogue record for this book is available from the British Library.

ISBN 1 84538 161 0

Written by Sue Nicholson
Designed by Susi Martin
Photographer Michael Wicks
Editor Paul Manning

Publisher Steve Evans
Creative Director Louise Morley
Editorial Manager Jean Coppendale

Printed and bound in China

The author and publisher would like to thank Millie and Emily
Sarah Morley for making the models.

Picture credits
CORBIS/Caroline Penn 6, /Kevin Fleming 19, /Richard Cummings 22
Getty Images/ Steve Bly/Stone 15, /Bridgeman Art Library 17
The Art Archive/Musée des Arts Africains et Océaniens/ Dagli Orti 13
Travelsite/Neil Setchfield 9, 11
Werner Forman/British Museum 21

Note to teachers and parents

The projects in this book are aimed at children at Key Stage 1 and are presented in order of difficulty, from easy to more challenging. Each can be used as a stand-alone activity or as part of another area of study. For example, the Celtic brooch could be linked to learning about the Celts in history.

While the ideas here are offered as inspiration, children should always be encouraged to work from their own imagination and first-hand observations.

All projects in this book require adult supervision.

Sourcing ideas

★ Encourage the children to source ideas from their own experiences as well as from books, magazines, the Internet, galleries or museums.

★ Prompt them to talk about different types of art they have seen at home or on holiday.

★ Use the 'Click for Art!' boxes as a starting point for finding useful material on the Internet.*

★ Suggest that each child keeps a sketchbook of his or her ideas.

Evaluating work

★ Encourage children to share and compare their work with others. What do they like best/least about it? If they did the project again, what would they do differently?

★ Help the children to judge the originality of their work and to appreciate the different qualities in others' work. This will help them to value ways of working that are different from their own.

★ Encourage the children by displaying their work.

* Website information is correct at the time of going to press. However, the publishers cannot accept liability for information or links found on third-party websites.

Contents

Words in bold, **like this**, are explained in the Glossary on page 24.

Getting started

This book will show you how to make amazing crafts from around the world. Here are some of the things you will need to get started:

Top tip
Don't forget to spread out some newspaper to work on, and wear an apron or an old shirt to keep your clothes clean.

Basic equipment
- Sketchpad, pencils and ruler
- Poster or **acrylic** paints
- Felt-tip pens
- Safety scissors
- **PVA** or other white glue
- Hole punch

Any extra items are listed with each project.

Paper
Start a collection of:
- Thick white paper or thin card
- Coloured paper
- Tissue paper
- Cardboard
- Silver foil

Craft foam
You can buy big sheets of coloured craft foam. Some craft shops sell bags of foam already cut into small squares.

Bits and bobs

Keep a big box full of things to decorate your crafts, for example:

★ Beads and buttons
★ Sequins and glitter
★ Scraps of tissue paper
★ Pieces of fabric, such as lace
★ Feathers, string, cord and wool

Salt and acrylic paints.

Paints and brushes

You will need:

- White **emulsion** paint
- Poster or acrylic paints
- A small brush for glue
- A medium-sized paintbrush
- A small, thin paintbrush

Glue

PVA glue is good for making things, but be careful not to get it in your eyes.

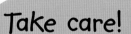

Take care!

Some projects involve cutting. Always ask an adult for help where you see this sign: ⚠

African cloth picture

In Benin, Africa, people tell stories in brightly coloured cloth pictures. You can make your own picture using **felt**.

A long time ago, cloth pictures like these hung behind the throne of the king of Benin.

You will need:
- Felt (black, red, yellow, orange)

Ask an adult to help you enlarge these animal shapes on a photocopier.

1 Draw an animal with felt-tip pen on the back of a piece of felt. Ask an adult to help you cut it out with scissors.

Click for Art!

To see traditional cloth pictures from Benin, visit **www.kidstoafrika.org/benin/tapestries**

Top tip

Cut scraps of different-coloured felt and glue them on your cut out animal shape.

2 Ask an adult to help you cut out a piece of black felt for your background. Make it at least 5cm bigger than your felt shape.

3 Cut out four strips of coloured felt 3cm wide to make a frame. Overlap the strips at each corner and glue them in place.

4 Glue your animal picture in the middle of the black background.

Carnival mask

Make yourself a colourful decorated mask like the ones worn at **carnival** time in Venice, Italy!

You will need:
- Thick cardboard
- Sequins, beads and glitter
- Ribbon or elastic

1 Photocopy the mask shape below. Ask an adult to help you cut out the shape, then draw around it onto cardboard.

2 Ask an adult to help you cut out the cardboard mask shape.

3 Make holes in the sides of the mask with a hole punch.

4 Paint the mask in bright colours. When it is dry, glue on sequins or beads. You can also paint glue in a pattern, then sprinkle silver or coloured glitter over it.

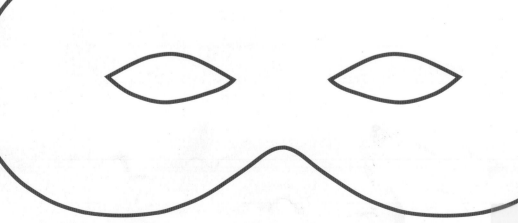

This person is wearing a traditional Venetian carnival mask.

5 Thread ribbon or elastic through the holes at the sides and tie the mask around your head.

Click for Art!

To read about Venetian masks and costumes, go to:
http://english.comune.venezia.it/turismo/feste/carnevale/en_maschere.asp

Arabian mosaic

In **Islamic** countries, such as Saudi Arabia, coloured tiles are arranged in **geometric** shapes to make beautiful **mosaic** patterns.

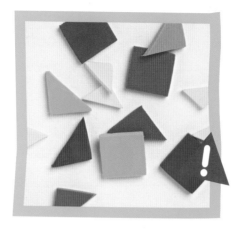

1 Ask an adult to help you cut foam squares into triangles, then cut some of the triangles into smaller triangles.

2 Glue a square into the middle of a piece of thin card. Glue four small triangle shapes around it.

You will need:
- Craft foam, cut into small squares
- Thin card

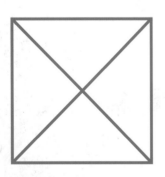

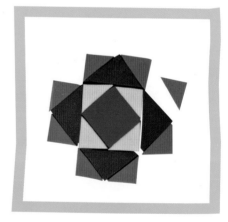

3 Add four large triangle shapes...

4 ... then eight small triangle shapes.

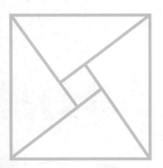

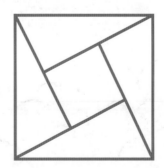

Try copying the shapes on the left to make exciting patterns of your own!

Islamic tiles with shapes arranged in a geometric pattern.

Click for Art!

To see an example of Islamic mosaic art, go to **www.metmuseum.org** and search on 'Mihrab'.

5 Finish off with eight large triangles to form a square.

Aboriginal painting

This project shows you how to paint a dot picture in the style of the Australian **Aboriginal** people.

1 Paint the whole of your paper pale yellow or orange. Leave to dry.

2 Ask an adult to help you copy the lizard shape below onto your picture. Paint it a rich, rusty red. Add wavy lines around it in dark orange or red and leave to dry.

3 Dip a cotton bud in white or yellow paint. Print rows of dots on the lizard's back and on some of the wavy lines.

You will need:
- Acrylic or poster paints in rich, warm colours
- Cotton buds

Click for Art!

For examples of Aboriginal dot paintings, go to **www.thebritishmuseum.ac.uk/compass/** and search on 'Aboriginal art'.

4 Paint large orange or red circles around the lizard. When the paint is dry, print black or brown and white or red dots on the circles.

Lively dot patterns and warm, earthy colours are typical of Aboriginal art.

Top tip
Arrange blobs of different-coloured paint in saucers. Use a different cotton bud for each colour.

Native American war bonnet

Here's how to make a **Native American** headdress using card, feathers, string and beads.

1 Ask an adult to help you cut a piece of cardboard 8cm wide and 12–15cm long. Punch two holes in each side of the band.

2 Tear newspaper into strips 3cm wide and 6cm long. Glue three layers of strips to the band to make it thicker.

3 While the glue is wet, push a pencil through the holes in the band. Leave to dry.

4 Paint the band with white emulsion. When dry, paint patterns and pictures on it.

You will need:
- Thick cardboard
- Newspaper
- White emulsion paint
- Feathers, string, ribbon and coloured beads

Click for Art!

To see a traditional Arapaho headdress, go to
www.nativeamericans.com/Arapaho.htm

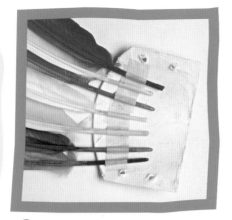

5 Glue or tape feathers behind the band so that they stick up from the top.

6 Thread ribbon through the holes of the band so you can wear it around your head. Thread beads onto the strings and knot the ends so they do not slide off.

A Native American today wearing a traditional headdress.

Celtic brooch

Make yourself a brooch in the style of the ancient **Celts**.

You will need:
- Cardboard
- A small cup
- Kitchen foil
- Tracing paper
- Black poster paint
- Cotton wool
- A safety pin
- Sticky tape

1 Draw around the rim of a cup on cardboard. Ask an adult to help you cut out the circle.

2 Cut out a square of kitchen foil, 4–5cm larger than the circle. Place the square over the circle and fold under the edges.

3 Choose a design and carefully trace over it with a soft pencil. Make the lines thick so the design stands out.

4 Place the tracing paper on the foil. Press hard over the lines with a pencil so that you make marks in the foil.

Top tip
You can also paint your design on the card circle with PVA glue and paint the brooch when the glue is dry. The gold brooch in the picture below has been made like this.

5 Rub black poster paint over the foil, then gently wipe it away with clean cotton wool so black paint is left in the grooves.

6 Fix a safety pin on the back of your brooch with sticky tape, so you can wear it. If you like, buy a gem from a craft shop to glue in the middle of your brooch.

Jewellery like this beautiful Celtic brooch is still made in Scotland and Ireland.

Click for Art!

For examples of Celtic brooches and bracelets, go to **www.thebritishmuseum.ac.uk/compass** and search on 'Celtic jewellery'.

17

Chinese paper dragon

At New Year, Chinese people dance in the street with huge paper and cloth dragons. Here's how to make a puppet dragon.

1 Trace the dragon's head and tail onto tracing paper, then onto thick cardboard. Ask an adult to help you cut out the shapes.

2 Paint both sides of a sheet of A4 paper bright red. When dry, fold the paper in half lengthwise and cut along the fold.

3 Fold the pieces of paper to form a **concertina**. Glue the two pieces of paper together to make one long piece for the dragon's body.

Ask an adult to enlarge these shapes on a photocopier.

Click for Art!

To learn about dragons in Ancient China go to **www.chinapage.com/dragon1.html**

The dragon dance is performed at Chinese New Year to bring good luck.

plastic 'wiggle eye'

4 Paint the dragon's head and tail in bright colours and glue on sequins, glitter and a plastic 'wiggle eye'.

5 Glue the head and tail to the dragon's body with PVA glue.

6 Glue or tape the chopsticks or lolly sticks to the head and tail of the dragon puppet.

Indonesian batik

Traditional **batik** uses hot wax and **dye** to make beautifully patterned fabrics. Here's a simple way to make a colourful batik flag.

You will need:
- Plain cotton cloth, such as calico
- Crimping shears
- A white wax crayon
- A small paintbrush
- Cold-water dye, fixative and salt
- Washing-up bowl and rubber gloves

1 Ask an adult to help you cut the cloth into a rectangle 25 x 40cm. Use pinking shears so that the edge does not fray.

2 Draw a picture on one side of the cloth with a soft pencil.

3 Go over your design with the white wax crayon. (The dye will only colour the parts that have NOT been covered with wax.)

Click for Art!

To find out about Indonesian batik, go to:
http://members.tripod.com/aberges/

Batik cloth is made in Indonesia, in Southeast Asia.

Using cold-water dye*

Wearing rubber gloves, dampen the cloth in clean water. Pour dye into water in an old bucket or washing-up bowl. Add 125 g of salt and cold-dye fixative. Stir well. Put the damp, unfolded cloth into the dye. Leave for one hour, stirring every 5 to 10 minutes. Rinse well in cold water.

*These instructions apply to Dylon® cold-water dye and fixative. For other brands, be sure to read the manufacturer's instructions.

4 Ask an adult to help you dye the cloth (see blue box above).

5 When the cloth is dry, glue a stick down one side on the back to make a flag.

Mexican Metapec sun

Mexican craftspeople make beautiful clay pottery. Here's how to make a **Metapec** clay sun to hang on your wall.

You will need:
- Air-drying clay
- A rolling pin
- A mixing bowl
- A blunt kitchen knife
- Bright acrylic or poster paints
- Paintbrushes
- Cord or string

A typical **Metapec** clay sun from Mexico.

1 Soften the clay in your hands then flatten it with a rolling pin. It needs to be about 1.5cm thick and a bit bigger than your mixing bowl.

2 Place a mixing bowl over the clay. Ask an adult to help you cut around the bowl with a blunt knife.

3 Make holes for the eyes and mouth. Make clay eyes and eyebrows, a nose and mouth, and stick them on with a little water.

Top tip
To make your sun look happy or surprised, make faces in the mirror and watch how your mouth and eyes change.

4 Make clay rays to go around your sun's face. Press them firmly into place or stick them on with a little water.

5 Push a pencil through the top of the sun to make a hole for the string.

6 Leave your sun to harden, then paint it in bright colours. Thread string through the hole at the top so you can hang it on the wall.

Top tip
To make your clay sun look shiny, paint it with PVA glue mixed with water. The glue looks white when wet, but will be clear and shiny when it is dry.